The apes are undoubtedly the animals that fascinate people the most—and the reason is not hard to see. Of all the world's creatures, they are closest to us in form and behavior. Like us, they can stand upright, they have fingernails and fingerprints, they have large brains, and they have expressive faces. Most of all, they have an obvious intelligence that both amuses us and puzzles us.

So great is the resemblance of the apes to man that we have called them anthropoid ("man-like") apes. The larger anthropoids—gorillas, orangutans, and chimpanzees—are called "great" apes. The smaller members of the group—gibbons and siamangs—are called the "lesser" apes.

Great apes can be very large. Gorillas have reached a height of 6 feet 2 inches (1.9 meters), and although chimpanzees are the smallest of the great apes, they can weigh more than 150 pounds (68 kilograms). Great apes can also live a long time—over 50 years for gorillas and chimpanzees, and perhaps even longer for orangutans. All apes live in forests, and only East African chimpanzees are known to leave the forest to spend time in open areas. The total range of apes is small: a belt across middle Africa and a few parts of Southeast Asia.

LOWLAND GORILLA (MALE AND FEMALE)
Gorilla gorilla gorilla

COMMON CHIMPANZEE
Pan troglodytes

The anatomy of apes is obviously like human anatomy in many ways. Like us, apes have two legs and two arms, five fingers and five toes, large heads with two forward-looking eyes, 32 teeth, ears that have the same kinds of wrinkles and lobes. And sometimes, the way that apes move their bodies, the postures and gestures they may use, can seem very human indeed.

These are all important similarities—but there are important differences as well. As a group, apes are made for life in the trees, while we are suited to life on the ground. Even the great gorilla, which has become so heavy that it must spend most of its time on the ground, has a body that is really shaped for climbing and swinging (young gorillas still do these things).

The arms of apes are always longer than their legs. Orangutans and gibbons have longer arms (in relation to the size of their bodies) than gorillas and chimpanzees. And this is only fitting, since these two apes spend more time swinging than the others, and longer arms make swinging easier.

With the hair removed, various skin colors are revealed for the different apes. Chimpanzee skin can range from black-brown to almost white on the body. Gorillas, gibbons, and siamangs have black or gray skin. And the gray skin of orangutans is often tinged with *blue*.

All apes are covered with thick hair that insulates their bodies and protects them from rain. But certain spots on the body are without hair. A typical chimpanzee has little or no hair on its face, upper chest, fingers and ears. The palms of the hands and soles of the feet are also bare. Gorillas have similar bare spots, while orangutans and gibbons are usually more fully covered.

WHITE-HANDED GIBBON
Hylobates lar

SIAMANG
Symphalangus syndactylus

BORNEAN ORANGUTANS
Pongo pygmaeus pygmaeus

PYGMY CHIMPANZEE, OR BONOBO
Pan paniscus

THE APES
ZOOBOOKS®

Apes are very strong. In the wild, they take on very little fat as a rule, and the energetic lifestyle of orangs, gibbons, and chimpanzees keeps them in very good shape. A massive gorilla, of course, walks around all day lifting the tremendous weight of its own body. In general, apes are many times stronger than human beings of similar size.

Although the bodies of all apes are similar in general pattern, the basic plan has been modified with each type of ape. A comparison of the hands and teeth of the lightest and the heaviest apes shows how nature has adapted itself to the life requirements of the different species . . .

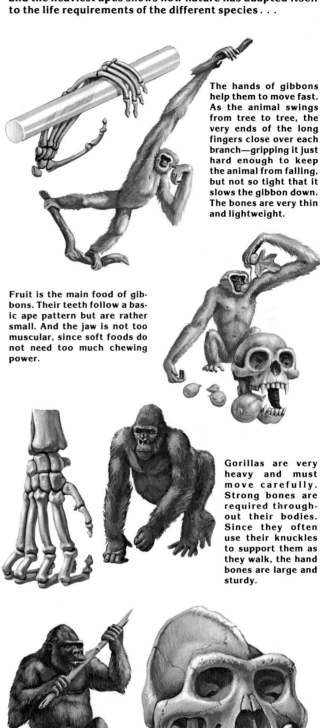

The hands of gibbons help them to move fast. As the animal swings from tree to tree, the very ends of the long fingers close over each branch—gripping it just hard enough to keep the animal from falling, but not so tight that it slows the gibbon down. The bones are very thin and lightweight.

Fruit is the main food of gibbons. Their teeth follow a basic ape pattern but are rather small. And the jaw is not too muscular, since soft foods do not need too much chewing power.

Gorillas are very heavy and must move carefully. Strong bones are required throughout their bodies. Since they often use their knuckles to support them as they walk, the hand bones are large and sturdy.

Tough and stringy plants are the major part of a gorilla's diet. Large muscles, running from the crest on the gorilla's skull to the lower jaw, supply plenty of power for chewing and grinding. The teeth are massive.

Most chimps eat only plants, but some hunt animals and eat meat. No other apes are hunters.

Since chimps spend as much as ⅓ of their day on the ground, they do quite a bit of walking. They prefer to walk on their feet and the knuckles of their hands, as shown below. Babies commonly ride from place to place by clinging to their mother's hair.

Play is important to chimpanzees of all ages. As with human children, young chimps learn behavior and skills through play. Mothers often spend hours playing with their babies. One favorite game is tickling.

When they want to carry something with two hands, chimps can walk upright. But they don't really feel comfortable in this position and cannot move very fast.

Excitement

Fear

Sadness

No two chimps look alike. Every face is different, and they have a very large number of different facial expressions.

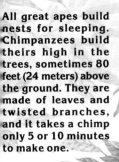

All great apes build nests for sleeping. Chimpanzees build theirs high in the trees, sometimes 80 feet (24 meters) above the ground. They are made of leaves and twisted branches, and it takes a chimp only 5 or 10 minutes to make one.

There are three different populations of chimpanzees, living in three separate areas of Africa. Eastern and Western chimps look much alike, but the smaller Pygmy chimps are darker in color. The pygmies live in an isolated area that is cut off from the other two groups by a wide river.

■ Eastern Chimpanzees
■ Western Chimpanzees
■ Pygmy Chimpanzees

Chimpanzees are the most social of the great apes. They like company, and temporary groups may include 45 or more chimps. Females and their young tend to wander from group to group, so the composition of groups is always changing. But males usually stay with a single group. When chimps arrive at a new place and meet old friends, they will sometimes hug and kiss in greeting as shown below.

Pygmy chimpanzees are probably the most intelligent of all animals after man. Scientific tests of their blood show that they are more closely related to man than any other animal. They live in smaller groups than other chimps and spend more time in trees.

As they grow older, chimpanzees often start to lose their hair. Females usually become more bald than males.

Among the tools that chimps have invented is a "leaf sponge," which they use to get drinking water out of tight places.

For a long time, man was thought to be the only tool user on earth. But now we know that quite a few animals use tools—and the chimpanzee is probably the best tool user of them all. Chimps in search of a meal use blades of grass to pull tasty termites out of their nests. They get honey out of bee hives with sticks.

Orangutans are only found in Southeast Asia, on the islands of Borneo and Sumatra. Unlike other apes, they live alone most of the time (with the exception of mothers, who may keep one or more of their young with them). This lonely lifestyle is probably related to the need that orangs have for large quantities of fruit.

Orangs are the largest animals in the world that survive mainly on fruit. In their lowland forest habitat, trees with ripe fruit are few and far between, and there may not be enough fruit on each tree to feed more than one or two orangs. So they spend most of their time alone, moving slowly through the trees from one food source to another.

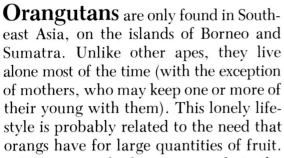

Orangutan mothers may keep their babies with them for as long as four years. The babies are carried almost all the time, clinging to the hair on their mother's back as she swings from place to place. In many cases, orangutan fathers leave after females become pregnant, and do not often see their children.

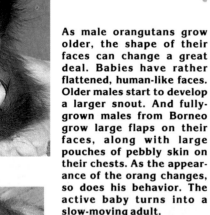

As male orangutans grow older, the shape of their faces can change a great deal. Babies have rather flattened, human-like faces. Older males start to develop a larger snout. And fully-grown males from Borneo grow large flaps on their faces, along with large pouches of pebbly skin on their chests. As the appearance of the orang changes, so does his behavior. The active baby turns into a slow-moving adult.

The younger an orangutan is, the higher he is likely to swing in the trees. Young orangs are both lightweight and active, so they are able to move on the highest levels. Older and heavier animals need sturdier branches to support their weight, and must be more careful about falling . . . so they are usually found on lower branches, or on the ground.

Although they are closely related, orangutans from Borneo and Sumatra can look very different. This is often easiest to see in the faces of mature males. Bornean males usually have large forward-curving flaps on their faces. They are likely to have balding, rather pointed heads. Sumatran males usually have flatter flaps and a flatter head, as well as a long flowing mustache.

SUMATRAN ORANGUTAN
Pongo pygmaeus abelii

As impressive as their cheek flaps can make them look, male Bornean orangutans do not usually grow to be extremely large in the wild. Their average weight is only 160 pounds (73 kilograms).

Sumatran orangutans are taller and more slender than their relatives in Borneo. Their hair may be longer and finer, and is sometimes lighter in color. Of all the great apes, they are perhaps the most "human" looking.

BORNEAN ORANGUTAN
Pongo pygmaeus pygmaeus

Past Range
Present Range

SUMATRA

BORNEO

The range of orangutans was once much larger than it is today. But, as man has destroyed forest to make room for farms and to harvest valuable timber, the orangs have been forced into smaller and smaller pockets.

To zoo keepers around the world, orangutans are known as "escape artists." They are very clever with their hands, and will often open cages just for the fun of it.

Gorillas are the largest of the great apes, but despite their great size they are generally shy and peaceloving. These gentle giants live together in rather small groups, with one mature male as the leader. There may be from 5 to 30 members in a group, but the average is 11. Young gorillas are small enough to swing in trees like the other apes, but heavier adults rarely leave the ground.

When they are not looking for food or eating, gorillas take it easy. They get up late and often go to bed early...and in between, they love to sunbathe and lie around.

In the wild, gorillas eat only plants. They spend about half of each day looking for food and eating it. Their diet can include leaves, bark, vines, bamboo shoots, and other tough and chewy materials.

Gorillas yawn like people. And they can shed tears. They are usually silent, but sometimes they will huff, cough, burp, and hiccough.

The undisputed boss of each gorilla group is a mature male with silver hair on his back. Silverbacks may be over 6 feet (1.8 meters) tall and may weigh between 300 and 400 pounds (136 and 181 kilograms). They have an arm span of at least 8 feet (2.4 meters), and are incredibly strong. It has been estimated, in fact, that a silverback has the strength of *4 to 8 strong men.* And yet, with all their brute strength, they are remarkably docile and gentle most of the time. They will patiently endure all kinds of playful torment from baby gorillas, for hours at a time, without losing their tempers.

LOWLAND GORILLA
Gorilla gorilla gorilla

MOUNTAIN GORILLA
Gorilla gorilla beringei

There are three basic types of gorillas—Western and Eastern Lowland Gorillas, and Mountain Gorillas. In the shapes of their bodies, all three types look much alike, but the heads of Lowland and Mountain Gorillas are quite different from each other. The hair on the head of a Lowland type is short and may be brown-orange in color. On a Mountain Gorilla, it is long and is as black as the rest of the body. Males of all types have crests on their heads, but Mountain Gorillas have higher crests.

■ Eastern Lowland Gorillas
■ Western Lowland Gorillas
■ Mountain Gorillas

Gorillas rarely stand up in the wild. They prefer to move about on all fours. When they do stand up, males often beat their chests. Interestingly, when mature males beat their chests, it is either a threat or a sign of curiosity. But when young gorillas do it, it is an invitation to play with them.

All known gorillas in the world are dark in color, except one. Discovered some years ago in West Africa, "Snowflake" now lives in the Barcelona Zoo. He is still a young gorilla, and zoo people hope that he will be able to sire a whole group of white gorillas.

Gibbons and siamangs are known as "the lesser apes," and scientists have placed them in a separate category from great apes. They are much smaller, weighing less than 17½ pounds (8 kilograms) as a rule. And unlike great apes, both sexes of each species are about the same size. These graceful little apes spend almost all of their time high up in the forest canopy, as much as 180 feet (55 meters) above the ground.

HOOLOCK GIBBON
Hylobates hoolock

Gibbons swing so rapidly that they sometimes appear to be flying. They can leap as far as 50 feet (15 meters) in a downward direction, and they are so well coordinated and quick that they can even catch flying birds!

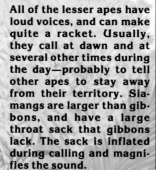

The basic gibbon social group is the family, made up of one male and one female, and as many as four of their young. Within each family, food is generously shared and fighting rarely occurs. But members of the same family will unite to drive off any strangers.

All of the lesser apes have loud voices, and can make quite a racket. Usually, they call at dawn and at several other times during the day—probably to tell other apes to stay away from their territory. Siamangs are larger than gibbons, and have a large throat sack that gibbons lack. The sack is inflated during calling and magnifies the sound.

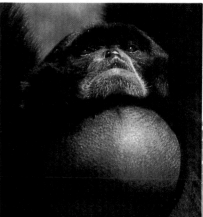

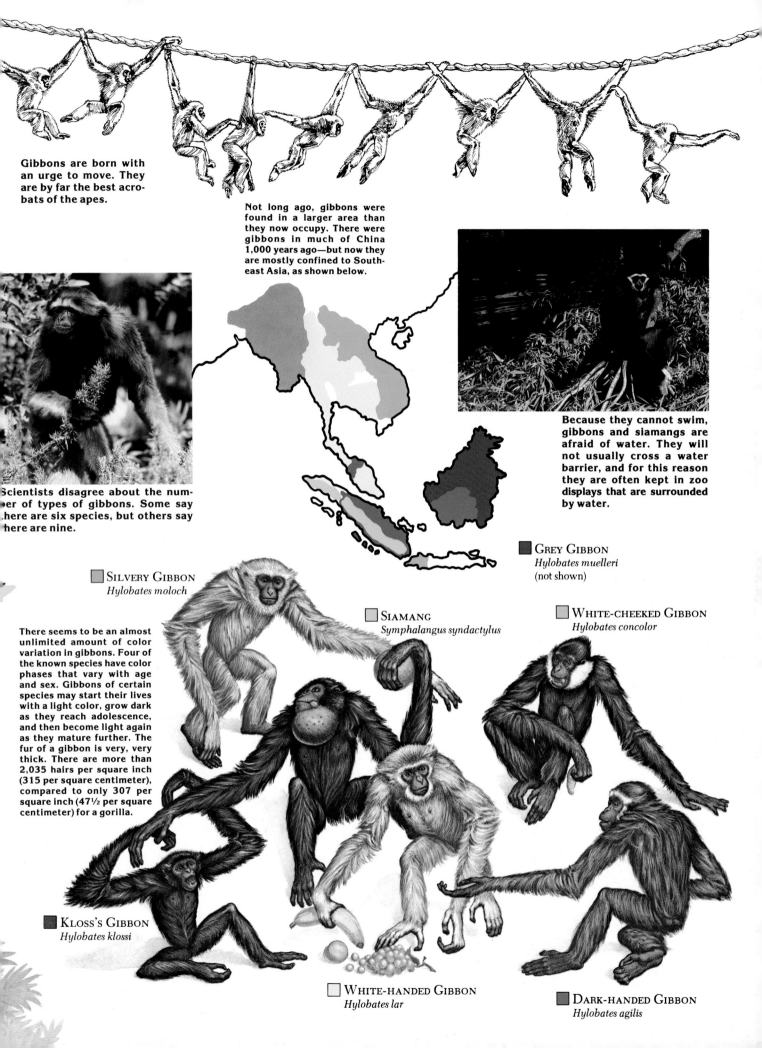

Gibbons are born with an urge to move. They are by far the best acrobats of the apes.

Not long ago, gibbons were found in a larger area than they now occupy. There were gibbons in much of China 1,000 years ago—but now they are mostly confined to Southeast Asia, as shown below.

Scientists disagree about the number of types of gibbons. Some say there are six species, but others say there are nine.

Because they cannot swim, gibbons and siamangs are afraid of water. They will not usually cross a water barrier, and for this reason they are often kept in zoo displays that are surrounded by water.

■ GREY GIBBON
Hylobates muelleri
(not shown)

■ SILVERY GIBBON
Hylobates moloch

■ SIAMANG
Symphalangus syndactylus

■ WHITE-CHEEKED GIBBON
Hylobates concolor

There seems to be an almost unlimited amount of color variation in gibbons. Four of the known species have color phases that vary with age and sex. Gibbons of certain species may start their lives with a light color, grow dark as they reach adolescence, and then become light again as they mature further. The fur of a gibbon is very, very thick. There are more than 2,035 hairs per square inch (315 per square centimeter), compared to only 307 per square inch (47½ per square centimeter) for a gorilla.

■ KLOSS'S GIBBON
Hylobates klossi

■ WHITE-HANDED GIBBON
Hylobates lar

■ DARK-HANDED GIBBON
Hylobates agilis

Apes have not benefited from their resemblance to man. On the contrary, people have traditionally seen their closest relatives as somehow ridiculous—and often menacing—parodies of human beings. Man has resented apes, even as he has been fascinated by them.

In the past 20 years, these old attitudes have started to change, as the result of scientific study. The myths about apes have been largely swept away. We now know that apes are intelligent, that they can master communication skills, and that they may even be able to think creatively. We are beginning to see how wonderful they are.

A lot of money has been made by presenting gorillas as monsters. Generations of children have been sold the image of the angry and dangerous gorilla. In reality, gorillas are among the most gentle creatures on earth.

DO NOT FEED

Some scientists claim that they have been able to teach apes to express themselves in sign language. Others say that the animals are simply imitating (or "aping") their teachers, and really don't understand the concepts necessary for human language. Above, Penny Patterson of the Gorilla Foundation signs to Koko: "How do you feel?" Koko signs back: "Fine."

Great apes are so closely related to man that they easily catch many of our diseases. And since they do not have the same resistance to these diseases that we have, they can even die from the complications of a common cold. This is why it is so important to keep human food, which might contain harmful germs, away from gorillas, chimps, and orangutans.

Rumors about large manlike creatures were brought back to Europe from Africa for centuries before any European finally saw a real gorilla in the 19th century. Without actual specimens to use for reference, artists during the 17th and 18th centuries drew apes as large and hairy people.

Chimpanzees have shown great enthusiasm for painting. When given paints and brushes, they produce paintings that are filled with bright color, and seem to express the joy of life. One scientist claims that chimps follow the same patterns in art that young humans do.

In creating horror stories for film audiences, the imaginations of writers have worked overtime on the gorilla. Dissatisfied with an ordinary ape, filmmakers dreamed up King Kong—20 times bigger than any gorilla that ever lived. All of man's ignorance about apes was wrapped up in one colossal and very destructive image.

The future of apes is up to us. All of the great apes are already on the endangered species list, and all of the lesser apes as well. Scientists who have studied them agree that all great apes will soon die out in the wild, unless steps are taken now to protect them.

Gorillas and orangutans appear to have no natural enemies, and chimpanzees have very few. Gibbons, because they move so fast and live so high up in the trees, are safe from any animal. Nothing could threaten any of the apes with extinction until man started hunting them, capturing them, and destroying the wild lands in which they live.

Today, hunting of apes is banned everywhere, and there are strict regulations concerning the capture of wild apes. But illegal hunting and trapping continues. And the greatest threat of all—the wholesale destruction of wild lands—grows greater every day. Tropical forests are being cut down faster today than ever before...at the rate of *one acre every second*, according to a recent report. At this incredible pace, the homes of many wild creatures—including apes—are simply disappearing.

Most endangered of the apes is the mountain gorilla. As recently as 1960, there may have been 15,000 of these majestic animals in East Africa. Today, there are less than 500.

The other apes are not much better off. No one is really sure how many pygmy chimpanzees survive in the jungles south of the Congo River—but it is probably less than 10,000. Fewer than 5,000 orangutans are thought to exist in scattered areas of Borneo and Sumatra. Populations of lowland gorillas and common chimpanzees are declining rapidly.

We must act *now* to help the United Nations, the World Wildlife Fund, zoos, and other organizations that are working to set aside wildlife preserves—places where the magnificent apes will be safe.

In recent years, some dedicated scientists have carried on long-term field studies of great apes. These have given us a great deal of information about biology and behavior that will help us to save the apes. Among the best-known researchers are Jane Goodall (chimpanzees), Birute Galdikas-Brindamour (orangutans), George Schaller (mountain gorillas), and Dian Fossey (mountain gorillas). At right, Dian Fossey with friends.

ZOO BOOKS®

Scientific Consultants

Frederick A. King, Ph.D.
Director
Yerkes Regional
Primate Research Center

Harold M. McClure, D.V.M.
Yerkes Regional
Primate Research Center

Richard Tenaza, Ph.D.
College of the Pacific

Art Credits

Inside Front Cover and Page One: Barbara Hoopes;
Pages Two and Three: Barbara Hoopes; Pages
Four and Five: James Teason and Mark Hallett;
Pages Six and Seven: James Teason; Page Seven:
Drawing by Mark Hallett; Page Ten: Barbara
Hoopes; Page Eleven: Lisa French and Barbara
Hoopes; **Page Twelve:** Middle, Lisa French;
Lower Left, Karl Edwards and Mark Hallett;
Page Thirteen: Top, Drawing by Walter Stuart;
Bottom, Lisa French; **Page Fifteen:** Upper Left,
Karl Edwards and Mark Hallett; Middle Right,
Drawing by Walter Stuart. All Maps by Andy
Lucas.

Photographic Credits

Front Cover: F. D. Schmidt/Zoological Society
of San Diego; **Page Four:** Lower Left, all three
photographs by Tom McHugh (Photo Research-
ers); **Page Five:** Upper Right, Charles Van Val-
kenburgh/Wildlife Education, Ltd.; Lower Right,
Tom McHugh (Photo Researchers); **Page Six:**
Lower Left, all three photographs by Ron Gar-
rison/Zoological Society of San Diego; **Pages
Eight and Nine:** Ira Block (Woodfin Camp);
Page Ten: Left, Peter Veit; Middle and Upper
Right, Charles Van Valkenburgh/Wildlife Edu-
cation, Ltd.; **Page Eleven:** Middle Right, Peter
Veit; Lower Right, James A. Sugar (Woodfin
Camp); **Page Twelve:** Lower Right, Ron Garri-
son/Zoological Society of San Diego; **Page Thir-
teen:** Upper Left, Ron Garrison/Zoological Soci-
ety of San Diego; Upper Right, Margot Conte
(Animals Animals); **Page Fourteen:** Lower Left,
Courtesy of Forrest Ackerman; Upper Right,
Courtesy of Circus World Museum, Baraboo,
Wisconsin; **Page Fifteen:** Upper Right, Ronald
H. Cohn/Gorilla Foundation; Lower Right, Mar-
tin Rogers (Woodfin Camp); **Page Sixteen and
Inside Back Cover:** Peter Veit.

Our Thanks To Barbara Shattuck (National
Geographic Magazine); Susan Hathaway (Zoo-
logical Society of San Diego); Michelle Robinson
(San Diego Zoo Library); Ken Stott; Dr.
Marshall (U.S. Fish and Wildlife Service);
Terry Maple (Georgia Institute of Technolo
Dian Fossey (Cornell University); Francine
terson (Gorilla Foundation); Lynnette Wexo.

Wildlife Education, Ltd.
930 West Washington St.
San Diego, CA 92103

ISBN 0-937934-03-8